ঌ Presentation Page ৎ

Presented by

Connie Clark
219 Chatuga Way
Loudon, TN 377742703

Presented to

❧ 123 Amazing Believers ❦
Every Christian Should Know

For information contact Belle Rive Publishers, 115 Penn Warren Drive, Suite 300, Box 321, Brentwood, Tennessee 37027.

Scripture quotations are from The Holy Bible, New Living Translation copyright © 1996 by Tyndale Charitable Trust. Used by permission of Tyndale House Publishers.

Printed in the United States of America.

ISBN # 0-9753409-3-X.

First Printing, September 2004

1 2 3 4 5 6 7 8 9 — 08 07 06 05 04

Now the church is not wood and stone,
but the company of people who believe in Christ
Martin Luther

One

Who: Lyman Abbott (1835-1922)

What: An influential nineteenth clergyman and editor, Abbott was born in Roxbury, Massachusetts and educated at New York University. He studied and practiced law from 1853 to 1859. He was ordained in 1860 and became pastor of the Congregational Church in Terre Haute, Indiana. In 1865 he was made secretary of the American Union Commission. He later became associate editor of the *Christian Union*. Among his many books were *Life and Letters of Paul* and *Jesus of Nazareth*.

Why: He stressed social ethics as a vital part of the Christian faith.

Two

Who: Joseph Addison (1672-1719)

What: Addison was the son of Reverend Lancelot Addison, Dean of Lichfield, England. He was educated at Oxford and developed poetic talent at an early age.

His literary contributions were made chiefly to various magazines. He is the author of five hymns, all of which appeared in the *Spectator* in 1712. At the time of his death he was contemplating a poetic version of the Psalms. "The piety of Addison," wrote a contemporary, "was in truth of a singularly cheerful kind. The feeling which predominates in all his devotional writings is gratitude; and on that goodness to which he ascribed all the happiness of his life he relied in the hour of death with a love which casteth out fear."

Why: His influence on others was gained through his charity, humbleness, and consistent walk of faith.

Three

Who: Eliza Agnew (1807-1883)

What: Born in New York City Agnew became a missionary to Ceylon in 1840 and was the first female missionary to that country. She became the head of the Central Boarding School for girls where she remained for 40 years. During her tenure more than

1,000 students came under her care, with many becoming Christians.

Why: She dedicated her life to bringing the Gospel message to the children of Ceylon.

Four

Who: Flaccus Albinus Alcuin (c. 735-804)

What: This advisor to Charlemagne was born in northern England and received his education at the cathedral school in York. In the late eighth century Alcuin became master of the School of the Palace at Aachen. His greatest contributions were to advance education across the empire, especially among the clergy, and to defend the church against the heresy of Adoptionism. He was a great scholar on the early church Fathers and wrote a number of hymns and Bible studies.

Why: He believed that an educated clergy would be the greatest weapon against heresy and paganism.

Five

Who: Alexander of Alexandria (d. 328)

What: Alexander defended orthodoxy against the heresy of Arianism. He called the synod in Alexandria where Arius, who believed that Jesus was a created being not fully equal with the Father, was condemned. After Alexander's death he was succeeded by the great Athanasius as bishop of Alexandria.

Why: He fought to preserve orthodoxy against Arianism, a very popular and widely preached heresy.

Six

Who: Henry Alford (1810-1871)

What: Alford, widely known as the author of *The Greek Testament with Notes*, was born in London in 1810. He wrote the following dedication in his Bible at the age of 16: "I do this day, in the presence of God and my own soul, renew my covenant with God, and solemnly determine henceforth to become his and to do his work as far as in me lies." He was educated at Trinity College, Cambridge, was ordained in 1833, and soon made a reputation as an eloquent preacher and sound biblical critic. He was appointed Dean of Canterbury in 1857, which distinction he held until the day of his death.

Why: He was living proof that it is never too early to dedicate your life to God.

Seven

Who: Ambrose (c. 340-397)

What: This Bishop of Milan was born in Gaul or modern day France. His father died when he was young and his family moved to Rome. Ambrose studied the law and was eventually appointed a civil governor. While still a new Christian the people of Milan elected him bishop when the previous bishop died. He began studying the Bible and theology in earnest and soon became a renowned preacher. His preaching was instrumental in the conversion of Augustine.

Why: He accepted the challenge of becoming a bishop, despite his lack of training, and dedicated his life to serving Christ and His Kingdom to the best of his ability.

Eight

Who: Jacob Ammann (c. 1644-c. 1711)

What: The founder of the Amish Mennonites, Ammann was an Anabaptist minister from Switzerland who strictly followed the practice of "avoidance." In 1693 he and 4,500 followers permanently left the Mennonite church, which disagreed with his views. Various attempts at reconciliation have proven unsuccessful.

Why: His convictions continue to influence the Amish to this day.

Nine

Who: Lancelot Andrewes (1555-1626)

What: Born near London, Andrewes was an eloquent Anglican preacher who was ordained in 1580 after graduating from Cambridge. He was the first appointee to translate the Authorized or King James Version of the Bible. He worked on 12 books in the Old Testament.

Why: His piety and convictions guided him during the daunting task of producing an accurate translation of the Bible that could be used by all people.

Ten

Who: Anselm (1033-1109)

What: Born in northern Italy, Anselm moved to England after the death of his mother. He entered a monastery and later became archbishop of Canterbury. His refusal to give the king authority over the church led to his banishment. During this time he wrote *Why God Man* where he stated that only the death of Christ could cancel the debt of sin. This was in opposition to the common belief at that time that Christ's death was a ransom paid to Satan. He wrote many other scholarly and devotional works during his lifetime.

Why: He wouldn't allow others, regardless of their authority, to sway him from the truth or from his convictions.

Eleven

Who: Anthony (c. 251-356)

What: The founder of Christian monasticism was born into a wealthy family in Egypt. After his parents died when he was 18 he became a hermit. For over 20 years he lived among the ruins of an ancient castle located on a mountaintop near the Nile. He would only come down a couple times each year for food. In 311, during a period of Roman persecution, he went to Alexandria to encourage the Christian community there. He soon returned to isolation until 335 when Athanasius contacted him to defend orthodoxy against Arianism. Afterward he again returned to his ascetic lifestyle until his death at the age of 105. His life became tremendously influential for many in the early centuries of the church.

Why: He believed that the things of this world held nothing compared to a life devoted fully to private communion with God.

Twelve

Who: Anthony of Padua (1195-1231)

What: Anthony was born in Portugal but moved to North Africa after joining the Franciscan order in 1220. Later he moved to Assisi where he met St. Francis, who was impressed with his gifts as a preacher and teacher. In 1229 he was made provincial of his order but continued writing and publishing sermons until his death. He is best known today as the patron saint of Portugal.

Why: He used his gifts humbly and in whatever manner he was asked for the service of the church.

Thirteen

Who: Thomas Aquinas (1225-1274)

What: Aquinas, perhaps the greatest of the medieval scholars, was born near Naples and studied at the Benedictine monastery of Monte Cassino. He later moved to Cologne, where he studied under the renowned intellectual Albertus Magnus, and then to Paris, where he received his doctorate. His masterpiece was *Summa Theologiae* (1265-1273) in which he attempted to prove such philosophical matters as the existence of God and address theological issues like the atonement. His theology was adopted as normative by the Roman Catholic Church at the Council of Trent (1545-1563).

Why: He used his great mind to logically address the weightiest matters of church doctrine.

Fourteen

Who: Jacob Arminius (1560-1609)

What: A Dutch theologian, Arminius studied and traveled widely during the years prior to his ordination in 1588. After receiving his doctorate he became a professor of theology at the University of Leyden. During this time Calvinism was made the official religion in Holland. He attempted to clarify Calvinism, especially with regard to the perception that humans were nothing more than puppets in the hands of God. He called for a national synod but died before this could take place. His theology, as well as his followers, were later condemned at the Synod of Dort in 1618.

Why: His beliefs continue to thrive in denominations like the Church of the Nazarene and other holiness groups.

Fifteen

Who: Francis Asbury (1745-1816)

What: The first Methodist bishop ordained in America, Asbury was born near Birmingham, England. He became a preacher after his conversion at the age of 13 and was later, at his own request, sent to America as a missionary in 1771. After the Revolutionary War Asbury was named superintendent and then bishop along with Thomas Coke in 1787. From that point Asbury worked tirelessly, traveling over 300,000 miles through forests, swamps, and wilderness and ordaining more than 4,000 preachers. Coke eventually returned to England, leaving Asbury to oversee Methodism in America alone. He succeeded brilliantly – there were nearly 200,000 Methodists in America at the time of his death.

Why: He gave away his meager belongings, never married, and worked under the harshest conditions to spread the Gospel.

Sixteen

Who: Athanasius (c. 296-373)

What: A young presbyter in the Alexandrian church during the ecumenical council in Nicea (325), Athanasius was the chief defender of Trinitarian doctrine against the heresy of Arianism. In 328 he became bishop after Alexander's death. He was banished four times for his stand against heresy by Arian Emperors. He was permitted to return each time. He wrote many works toward the end of his life defending the deity of Christ and affirming that anti-Trinitarianism is the most dangerous enemy of orthodoxy.

Why: He upheld the truths of Christianity against those who would have introduced heresy into the church.

Seventeen

Who: Aurelius Augustine (354-430)

What: One of the church's great theologians, Augustine converted to Christianity at the age of 33 due largely to the influence of his devout mother, Monica. His father, a prominent citizen in Numidia, North Africa sent Augustine to the finest schools in that city and in Carthage where he studied rhetoric. As a teacher he traveled from Carthage to Rome to Milan. His search for truth led him to study the ancient Greek philosophers, dualistic Manichaeism, and Skepticism. In Milan he heard Ambrose preach and, after studying the Scriptures, he converted to the faith of his mother in 381. She died shortly afterward. He returned to North Africa and entered a monastery in Hippo. In 395 he was chosen as bishop, a position he held until his death. His powerful writings served to defend the faith against the many popular heresies of that time including the Donatists, the Pelagians, and the Manichaeans. His seminal works include *The City of God*, a philosophy of Christian history; the

Enchiridion, a theological work; and *Confessions*, which told of his conversion.

Why: His influence extends to this day in both Roman Catholic and Protestant theologies.

Eighteen

Who: Gladys Aylward (1902-1970)

What: Aylward was a London parlor maid whose application to become a missionary to China was rejected by her local mission board. Despite this rejection, she saved her money and paid her own way in 1932. Along with another woman, Jeannie Lawson, she opened an inn where she taught the Bible and shared the Gospel. In 1940, during the Japanese invasion of China, she led 100 children to safety during a heroic journey through a mountain passage. She nearly died from the experience. In 1953 she opened an orphanage in Taiwan.

Why: She didn't allow the barriers thrown up by others to keep her from the ministry she knew God had called her to.

Nineteen

Who: Johann Sebastian Bach (1685-1750)

What: A master organist and composer, Bach was born in Eisenach, Germany to a family of noted musicians. Although he was proficient in various subjects by the age of 14 – including Latin, Greek, rhetoric, and theology – his main interest was in music. In 1709 he became a court musician at Weimer. His compositions numbered in the hundreds and included orchestral and vocal works as well as music for the organ, the instrument for which he is most famous. A devout Lutheran, most of his music was written for the church. He became blind in his later years but miraculously recovered his sight shortly before his death.

Why: His stunning compositions are unmatched in their brilliance and continue to inspire believers to this day.

Twenty

Who: Sabine Baring-Gould (1834-1924)

What: Baring-Gould, an English clergyman, was born in Exeter, England and was educated at Clare College,

Cambridge. His prose works included *Lives of the Saints* in fifteen volumes, 1872-1877. He was the author of a number of fine hymns, the best known of which is "Onward, Christian soldiers."

Why: His hymns and sermons stressed his conviction that Christians need not fear the snares of Satan since Christ has utterly defeated him.

Twenty-one

Who: Donald Grey Barnhouse (1895-1960)

What: Barnhouse, a writer and pioneer in Christian radio, graduated from the University of Chicago and Princeton Theological Seminary. He also studied in Europe where, for a time, he was a pastor and teacher in France. In 1927 he returned to the United States to begin a 33-year pastorate at Philadelphia's Tenth Presbyterian Church. Here he began his radio ministry, which focused primarily on the book of Romans; wrote more than 30 books, including *God's Method for Holy Living*; and served as the director of the Stony Brook School for Boys.

Why: He used his superior education and keen mind to make the truths of Scripture, particularly Pauline theology, accessible to a mass audience.

Twenty-two

Who: Karl Barth (1886-1968)

What: A Swiss theologian, Barth was the founder of the neo-orthodox school of theology. He studied at various universities in Germany and became a liberal pastor for 12 years in Switzerland. After seeing first hand the inherent sinfulness of humanity during the First World War he began studying Scripture and theologians like Calvin and Kierkegaard. Eventually he abandoned liberal theology. In his multi-volume *Church Dogmatics* he detailed his beliefs, which included the ideas that God is transcendent, and that humanity is separated from God due to sin – a condition that can only be resolved when the Holy Spirit reconciles us to God through Christ.

Why: His theology was, in many ways, universalist but was much more Christ-centered than the liberalism that reigned among scholars during the late 19th and early 20th centuries.

Twenty-three

Who: Richard Baxter (1615-1691)

What: Baxter, a Puritan minister and voluminous author of the seventeenth century, wrote the devotional masterpiece *Call to the Unconverted and his Saint's Everlasting Rest*. At 25 he entered the ministry and was appointed to the parish of Kidderminster (1640). Here he remained until "for conscience' sake" he, along with many other Nonconformist clergy, was driven out by the "Act of Uniformity" passed in 1662. He ceased to preach but was caught holding family prayers "with more than four persons." He was arrested and imprisoned for six months. When released he lived in retirement until 1672 when the "Act of Indulgence" gave him liberty to preach and to publish again.

Why: He refused to be silenced by the authorities and preached the Gospel despite the personal costs he paid.

Twenty-four

Who: Thomas à Becket (c. 1118-1170)

What: Becket, the legendary medieval archbishop of Canterbury, was born and educated in London. He was sent by the church to Bologna to study law and was named, in 1154, chancellor of England by Henry II. After serving admirably, he was named archbishop of Canterbury in 1162. He dedicated his life to the church and, rejecting the luxuries he had enjoyed as a state official, became a devout and pious priest. By claiming that the church was not answerable to the state his former friend Henry, a nationalist, turned against him. He fled to France in 1164 but returned in 1170 when Henry promised his safety. Later that year he was murdered by some of Henry's knights in the Cathedral of Canterbury.

Why: His bravery and unflinching allegiance to the church has inspired numerous books, at least one film, and a renowned play by T. S. Eliot.

Twenty-five

Who: Bede (c. 673-735)

What: The Venerable Bede, an English monk and historian, was a brilliant scholar who was named a deacon at 19 and became a priest at 30. He wrote a number of commentaries, hymns, and historical works – including the seminal *Ecclesiastical History of the English Nation* (731).

Why: His writings are a valuable resource for historians and are an informational link to the key events of the medieval church.

Twenty-six

Who: Lyman Beecher (1775-1863)

What: Beecher was born at New Haven, Connecticut, the descendant of one of the founders of the New Haven colony. In 1797 he graduated from Yale, having studied under Timothy Dwight. He preached in Presbyterian and Congregational churches in Connecticut, Massachusetts, and New York before accepting the pastorate of the Second Presbyterian church of Cincinnati. Here he became president of the newly established Lane Theological Seminary. He was a well-known opponent of Unitarianism, an eloquent preacher, an advocate of temperance, and the father of seven sons who became Congregational ministers and two daughters who became famous writers, especially Harriet who wrote *Uncle Tom's Cabin*.

Why: His style of preaching and the causes he fought for influenced preachers for several generations.

Twenty-seven

Who: Bernard of Clairvaux (c. 1090-1153)

What: Bernard, an eminent monk, theologian, scholar, preacher, and poet, was born in Burgundy, France. Aletta, his mother, was a pious woman and consecrated her son to God from his birth. Being naturally fond of seclusion, meditation, and study he sought a home in the cloister. At 22 he entered the small monastery of Citeaux and later founded and made famous that of Clairvaux. Kings and popes sought his advice since his enthusiasm and impassioned eloquence were all but irresistible. Luther greatly admired him and thought him "the greatest monk that ever lived." His published works are in five folio volumes.

Why: His wisdom and pious devotion influenced the church for centuries.

Twenty-eight

Who: Horatius Bonar (1808-1889)

What: Bonar, a distinguished Presbyterian minister, was born in Edinburgh, Scotland. He was educated at the University of Edinburgh, was ordained in 1837, and became a minister of the Established Church at Kelso. He later became one of the founders of the Free Church of Scotland. He was a voluminous writer of sacred poetry until his death.

Why: His devotional works greatly influenced the church in his day and his hymns continue to be sung in Protestant churches.

Twenty-nine

Who: Winfrid Boniface (680-755)

What: Boniface, the apostle of Germany, was born in Devonshire, England and became a monk after studying grammar and theology at Exeter. For a time he was a missionary to Frisia, an area comprised mostly of the modern Netherlands. In 719 Pope Gregory II commissioned him to evangelize Germany where he preached successfully for about three years. In 722, after converting a number of chieftains, Gregory consecrated him bishop. From this point he expanded his mission by founding numerous churches and monasteries and bringing in a number English missionary monks and nuns. After being named archbishop in 732 he organized the churches in Bavaria into the four bishoprics of Regensburg, Freising, Salzburg, and Passau. In 741 Pope Zacharias made him legate and charged him with the reformation of the whole Frankish church. In 753 he returned to Frisia to continue the evangelistic efforts he had begun many years earlier. Sadly, in 755, he and a group of missionaries were killed by a band of pagans who opposed their efforts.

Why: He died bringing the Gospel to the German people but his message took root and the churches, schools, and monasteries he founded had a great and lasting impact.

Thirty

Who: William and Catherine Booth (1829-1912 & 1829-1890)

What: The Booths were the founders of the Salvation Army. William was born near Nottingham, England into an Anglican family. He converted to Methodism and began a ministry of street preaching and attending to the needs of the sick and poor. Catherine was born in Derbyshire, England. She was very sickly as a child and young woman and seldom left home. She moved to London with her parents in 1844 where she met and later married William. Together they began a vital ministry among the lower classes in East London. They founded what was first called the East London Christian Revival Society and later the Salvation Army. Catherine died of cancer but not before she had worked tirelessly to secure the passage of laws that improved the lives of women and children. William lived another two decades and saw his organization, well known for its military themes and disciplines, spread to 55 countries. During his lifetime he traveled over five million miles and preached about 60,000 sermons. The Salvation Army continues to thrive and provide help for those in need, in Christ's name, throughout the world.

Why: They worked together as a couple to found one of the most influential and respected charitable organizations in the world.

Thirty-one

Who: Edward McKendree (E. M.) Bounds (1835-1913)

What: A Methodist minister and renowned devotional writer, Bounds was born in Missouri and studied law as a young man. After passing the bar he practiced for a short period before accepting a pastorate in Brunswick, Missouri. When the Civil War broke out he refused to serve and was imprisoned. Later he traveled as a chaplain with the Fifth Missouri regiment. After the war he served as pastor at various churches in Missouri, Tennessee, and Alabama and worked as an editor at the *Christian Advocate*. He retired to Georgia and spent the last years of his life writing various books, primarily on the subject of prayer. He was known to pray for several hours each day.

Why: His books on prayer, especially *Purpose in Prayer* and *Power through Prayer*, have become classics.

Thirty-two

Who: David Brainerd (1718-1747)

What: Brainerd was born in Haddam, Connecticut. At the age of 14 he was orphaned. He studied for nearly three years (1739-1742) at Yale but was expelled for criticizing the spiritual depth of one of the tutors. He prepared for the ministry and became licensed to preach in 1742. Early in 1743 he decided to devote himself to missionary work among the

Indians. Supported by the Scottish Society for Promoting Christian Knowledge, he worked first at Kaunaumeek, an Indian settlement near Stockbridge, Massachusetts, and later among the Delaware Indians in Pennsylvania (near Easton) and New Jersey (near Cranbury). His frail health and tireless efforts as a missionary led to his early death. He died at the home of his friend, Jonathan Edwards, in Northampton, Massachusetts. His *Journal* was published in two parts in 1746. In 1749 Jonathan Edwards published *An Account of the Life of the Late Reverend David Brainerd*, which has become a missionary classic.

Why: His brief but inspiring life and his writings have roused countless young people to dedicate their lives to mission work.

Thirty-three

Who: Elizabeth Barrett Browning (1809-1861)

What: Browning, scarcely less famous as a poet than her illustrious husband, Robert Browning, was born in London. In 1846 she and her husband moved to Italy where she lived until her death. In all literature there is no parallel case where husband and wife have each attained such distinction as poets. Beginning at eight years of age to write, she produced during the forty years of her literary life countless poems of artistic beauty that reflected her Christian faith.

Why: Her literary stature greatly influenced other Christian writers, hymnists, and poets.

Thirty-four

Who: Martin Bucer (1491-1551)

What: A German Protestant reformer, Bucer entered the Dominican order in 1506. He was sent to Heidelberg for further study where he became acquainted with the works of Erasmus and was present at a debate between Luther and a group of Catholic theologians. His friendship via correspondence with Luther and his study of the Bible led to his conversion to the Protestant faith. He abandoned his order in 1521 and soon afterward married a former nun. In 1523 he accepted a pastoral position in Strasbourg where he remained for 25 years. He was a brilliant organizer and set up charitable organizations, established a school and seminary, wrote liturgies and hymns, and served as a mediator between Lutheran and Calvinist groups. His opposition to an effort to unite Catholics and Protestants placed his life in danger and he fled to England at the invitation of Thomas Cranmer. Here, in 1549, he was appointed regius professor of divinity at Cambridge where he wrote and taught until his death.

Why: His fervor in maintaining that an insurmountable gulf exists between Protestant and Roman Catholic theology reinforced the convictions of many other Reformers.

Thirty-five

Who: John Bunyan (1628-1688)

What: A Baptist preacher and writer Bunyan grew up in Bedford, England, joined the army as a teenager, and later became a tinker, the trade of his father. He married a pious believer who led him to Christ. After his baptism he joined the Baptist church and began preaching. Since he had not received permission from the Established Church he was arrested and thrown into jail in 1660. His family fell into severe poverty during this time and he was rarely permitted to see them. Yet, despite these circumstances, he wrote one of the great classics of literature, *The Pilgrim's Progress*, while imprisoned. The Act of Pardon freed him in 1672 and he became pastor of the Bedford Baptist Church, a congregation he served until his death. He wrote other books including *The Holy War* and *Grace Abounding*.

Why: His allegory *The Pilgrim's Progress* is considered one of the great works of Christian literature and was often one of only two books, along with the Bible, that families owned for over 200 years until the early 20th century.

Thirty-six

Who: John Calvin (1509-1564)

What: A French Reformer and theologian, Calvin was the son of a lawyer who planned for him to become a priest. In 1523 he began studies at the University of Paris until his father changed his mind and sent him to the University of Orleans to study law. After his father's death in 1531 he abandoned law and went to Paris to study humanities. Here he had a "sudden conversion," as he would later describe it, and left the Catholic Church to become a Protestant leader and preacher. His outspokenness and brilliant mind got him in trouble in Paris so he and a companion, Nicholas Cop, left the city; eventually ending up in Strasbourg. Here, in 1536, he published *Institutes of the Christian Religion*, which stressed the sovereignty of God, a limited atonement, predestination, and irresistible grace. His travels took him to Geneva, Switzerland where he eventually, after a series of conflicts with the Catholic leadership and others, established the city as the "Rome of Protestantism." He ran the city with strict authority and engaged in organizing nearly every aspect of its civic affairs. He remained here until his death.

Why: He, along with Luther and Knox, is considered one of the three greatest figures of the Reformation and his influence can be seen to this day in the various denominations that embrace his theology, including Presbyterian and Reformed churches.

Thirty-seven

Who: William Carey (1761-1834)

What: Considered the "father of modern missions," Carey was born in Paulersbury, England to a poor weaver. As a young man he worked as an apprentice to a shoemaker but spent his spare time studying for the ministry. Amazingly, while still a teenager, he was able to read the Bible in six languages. This gift for language would serve him well as a missionary. In 1787 he became pastor of a Baptist church where, in 1792, he preached a sermon with the famous line, "Expect Great Things from God, Attempt Great Things for God." He helped organize the Baptist Missionary Society and became one of the group's first members to go abroad when he went to India in 1793. He suffered greatly during the early years of his ministry due to financial setbacks, the death of his children, and the mental illness of his wife. In 1799 he was able to purchase a small indigo plantation and it was from here that he started his first successful mission. Opposition from the East India Company forced him to shut down his operation, however, so in 1800 he moved to Serampore where he and other missionaries preached, taught, and started Serampore Press to distribute Christian literature. In 1831 Carey was appointed professor of Oriental languages at Fort William College in Calcutta, a position he held for 30 years until his death. During this time he was largely responsible for translating the Bible into 36 dialects, making the Scriptures available to over 300 million people.

Why: His philosophy toward missions – missionaries and natives should live equally and missionaries should be self-sustaining – revolutionized the work of mission societies and led to field successes previously unmatched.

Thirty-eight

Who: Amy Carmichael (1867-1951)

What: Born in Northern Ireland and educated at Wesleyan Methodist Boarding School, Carmichael grew up in a wealthy and well-connected family. Yet, despite her privileged circumstances, she dedicated her life to missions and went to Japan in 1893. Poor health forced her to return to England but in 1895 she was sent by the Church of England to South India. Here she remained until her death. She adopted Indian dress and began working among the young girls who had been dedicated to lives of servitude at Hindu temples. She rescued many of them and established a home that eventually accepted both boys and girls. After an accident in 1931 that left her unable to walk she began writing devotional books, including *Mimosa* and *Lotus Buds*, that were published in many languages.

Why: Her efforts on behalf of the slave girls of South India led to protective laws and inspired many women to become missionaries.

Thirty-nine

Who: George Washington Carver (c. 1864-1943)

What: Born near Carthage, Missouri of slave parents, Carver became one of the great educators and scientists of the early 20th century. He worked his way through Iowa State College of Agriculture and Mechanic Arts, graduating in 1894. He accepted a position with the Department of Agricultural Research at Tuskegee Institute in Alabama and began a 50-year career that led to many developments in the uses of such crops as peanuts and sweet potatoes. A Sunday school teacher and member of the Presbyterian Church, he believed that all of his discoveries came directly from God.

Why: His stature as an African-American scientist in pre-Civil Rights America was nearly unprecedented.

Forty

Who: Lewis Sperry Chafer (1871-1952)

What: Born in Ohio and educated at Oberlin Conservatory and College, where he studied under C. I. Scofield, Chafer was a Presbyterian educator and evangelist who is best-known for founding the Evangelical Theological College – later renamed Dallas Theological Seminary. He spent most of his life here writing, teaching, and serving as president.

Why: He was very influential in promoting and preserving conservative theology and dispensational doctrine.

Forty-one

Who: John Chrysostom (c. 347-407)

What: Born in Syria, Chrysostom studied rhetoric under the famed teacher Libanius. After his mother's death he entered a monastery near Antioch in 373 and remained there until about 381. That year he was named deacon of Antioch, a position he held for five years. In 386 he became the chief preacher in the city, due primarily to his great oratorical skills (*Chrysostom* means "golden mouthed"). In 398 he was named archbishop of Constantinople. Here he condemned the immorality of Queen Eudoxia which led to his banishment. He continued to care for the spiritual lives of the church through correspondence and contacts with friends. He died in exile.

Why: His commentaries on the Bible along with his faithfulness during persecution made him a leading figure in the early church.

Forty-two

Who: Adam Clarke (c. 1762-1832)

What: A Methodist minister, commentator, and theologian, Clarke was born in Ireland and, after receiving a very limited education, was apprenticed to a linen manufacturer. He eventually entered a school founded by John Wesley and was soon appointed, in 1782, as a Methodist circuit rider. His popularity as a preacher was great, and his influence in the denomination is indicated by the fact that he was three times (1806, 1814, and 1822) chosen to be president of the British conference. His most significant work, *Commentary on the Holy Scriptures*, was published in eight volumes and took more than 45 years to complete.

Why: His commentary, now available primarily in an abridged form, was an influential work that set a high standard for all commentaries that followed.

Forty-three

Who: Columba (c. 521-597)

What: The renowned Irish Celtic missionary was probably born in County Donegal. His father was a member of the reigning family in Ireland and his mother was descended from royalty. During his youth the church in Ireland grew considerably and numerous monasteries were founded. Columba embraced the monastic life and became a deacon and priest in about 551. In 563 he left Ireland, accompanied by twelve disciples, and went on a mission to northern Britain. They landed first on Iona, a small island off the coast of Scotland, where they erected a church and a monastery. About 565 they began evangelizing the heathen kingdom of the northern Picts. They succeeded in converting the king and many of his subjects. Eventually the whole of northern Scotland was converted by the labors of Columba and his disciples and numerous churches and monasteries were established. Iona remained the primary center for oversight and missionary training. He died beside the altar of a church he had founded during his midnight devotions.

Why: His courage and determination, along with his tremendous planning skills, led to the conversion of the unreached tribes of Scotland.

Forty-four

Who: Constantine the Great (c. 280-337)

What: Constantine, the first Christian Roman Emperor, was installed by Roman troops in 306 after distinguishing himself in the Egyptian and Persian wars during the reign of Diocletian. Maxentius initially challenged him for the throne; however in 312, at Milvian Bridge, Constantine defeated Maxentius after seeing a vision of a cross in the sky with the inscription "By this conquer." In 313 Constantine signed the Edict of Milan, which made Christianity a legal religion. An insightful administrator he knew that one of the best ways to govern such a large empire was to unite his subjects under the banner of one faith. He made Christianity the official religion and began placing believers in high positions, establishing schools, building churches, and setting aside Sunday as a day for church attendance. He also called the ecumenical council in Nicea in 325 to settle the disputes over the person and nature of Jesus. Despite all of this he was not baptized until shortly before his death.

Why: He ended the persecutions and made Christianity the official religion of the Roman Empire – actions that together launched the explosive growth of the faith.

Forty-five

Who: Miles Coverdale (1488-1568)

What: An English Bible translator, Coverdale was born in Yorkshire and studied philosophy and theology at Cambridge. He was ordained priest at Norwich in 1514 and then entered an Augustinian monastery. In 1528 he left the monastery to begin preaching and working on a translation of the Bible. In 1535 he published the first complete English translation, called the "Great Bible." This was followed by a revision in 1540. The remainder of his life was eventful but did not have the same impact. Between 1543 and 1547 he served as a Lutheran minister in Strasbourg. As the Protestant bishop of Exeter he was imprisoned by Queen Mary but escaped to Denmark. When he returned, during Elizabeth's reign, he was not reinstated to the bishopric but, instead, spent most of the remainder of his life as a minister in London.

Why: His English translation was the first to contain the entire Bible and it laid the foundation for the subsequent work of translators.

Forty-six

Who: William Cowper (1731-1800)

What: Cowper was born in Hertfordshire, England. His father, Reverend John Cowper, was a chaplain to George II. He spent ten years in Westminster School and then began reading law; abandoning it for literature after a very brief practice. He became the most distinguished poet of the English language in the latter half of the 18th century. Despite this he suffered from debilitating depression. In 1767 he moved to Olney, the home of John Newton. Cowper was a constant and prayerful attendant at Newton's church services; especially his cottage prayer meetings, for which nearly all of his hymns were written at Newton's request. The Olney Hymns, 1779, was their joint production; 78 of them coming from Cowper.

Why: His resolve and willingness to accomplish great things for God despite emotional burdens has long served as a source of encouragement for those who suffer from depression.

Forty-seven

Who: Thomas Cranmer (1489-1556)

What: Cranmer, the first Protestant archbishop of Canterbury, was born in Nottinghamshire, England and studied at Jesus College, Cambridge for eight years. In 1523 he became a university preacher. When the issue of Henry's divorce from Catherine arose, he was appointed archbishop after making the case that it was a matter that should be decided by theologians rather than by Rome. As archbishop he annulled the marriage and validated the crowning of Anne Boleyn. He instituted Protestant reforms, including the introduction of a Bible in the common vernacular, known as "Cranmer's Bible." After Henry's death, and during the reign of Edward VI, he did much to firmly establish the Church of England by writing or commissioning the First and Second Prayer Books and the Forty-two Articles (later the Thirty-nine Articles). When the Catholic Mary became queen in 1153, he was arrested and thrown into the tower in London. He was burned at the stake after first recanting but then later affirming his Protestant views.

Why: He was the chief architect of the Church of England, a cornerstone for many Protestant denominations.

Forty-eight

Who: Frances Jane (Fanny) Crosby Van Alstyne (1820-1915)

What: Crosby was the most prolific and perhaps the most popular writer of Sunday school hymns that America has ever produced. She was born in Putnam

County, New York. When only six weeks old she lost her eyesight. Her first poem was written when she was eight. At the age of 15 she entered the Institution for the Blind in New York City, where she spent seven years as a pupil and 11 years (1847-1858) as a teacher. In 1844 she published a volume entitled *The Blind Girl and Other Poems*. In 1851 she accepted Christ and joined the Methodist Episcopal Church. In 1858 she married Alexander Van Alstyne, who was also, like she, blind, had been a teacher in the Institution, and was possessed of rare musical talent. During her lifetime she wrote more than six thousand hymns.

Why: Her extraordinary catalog of music, composed despite her physical impairment, has blessed countless believers for many generations.

Forty-nine

Who: Thascius Caecilius Cyprian (c. 200-258)
What: The son of a wealthy Roman officer, Cyprian led a privileged life as a young man and received an excellent education. As an adult he became a Christian

and turned his back on his family's affluence to embrace the study of the Scriptures and asceticism. In about 250 he was named bishop of North Africa, after serving for a year as presbyter in Carthage. This was a difficult time in the church as severe persecutions raged and various cults and heresies arose. He went into hiding to escape capture but maintained contact with his churches through regular correspondence. In 251 he returned to Carthage to preside over the affairs of the church. In 257, during a persecution by Valerian, he was tried and executed.

Why: His writings set Peter as the Apostle whom all bishops succeed, establishing a church government and order of unity that continues to this day.

Fifty

Who: John Nelson Darby (1800-1882)

What: The founder of the Plymouth Brethren, Darby was born in London and graduated from Trinity College. He began practicing law in 1825 but gave it up to serve as a curate in the Church of Ireland. He began to have doubts about issues like denominationalism, the role of pastors, and the relationship between Christians and the church. He gathered a group of worshipers to meet in Plymouth called the Brethren, later identified by the town from which they arose. He traveled extensively in France and Switzerland, establishing churches in many regions. He was a prolific writer and hymnist and he set up churches throughout Europe, the South Pacific, and North America.

Why: His efforts established the Plymouth Brethren and the various denominations and sects that have broken off of it in the last 150 years.

Fifty-one

Who: Philip Dodderidge (1702-1751)

What: Doddridge, one of the most distinguished Congregational ministers of the eighteenth century, was the youngest of 20 children. He entered the ministry at the age of 19. In 1729 he moved to Northampton where he became pastor of the Dissenting Church and also organized and conducted a theological school for young preachers. As many as 150 students studied theology with him during the 20 years he was there. His *Family Expositor* and *Rise and Progress of Religion in the Soul* were translated into many languages. He died of consumption in Lisbon, Portugal.

Why: He trained many preachers who, in turn, had a great influence on 18th century Congregational churches.

Fifty-two

Who: Alexander Duff (1806-1878)

What: The first missionary to India from the Church of Scotland, Duff established the University of Calcutta in 1830. Within ten years it had grown to nearly 1,000 students. Ill health forced him to return to Scotland in 1834 for six years, during which time he raised funds and promoted the work of other missionaries. During the next few years he suffered several setbacks due to divisions in the Church of Scotland and he eventually lost the right to minister from his school. He spent several years traveling the globe to campaign for missions, including the United States where he had a great impact and inspired many to become missionaries. He retired to Scotland in 1864 and spent the rest of his life teaching theology, serving as a moderator in the Free Church, and writing and speaking about the importance of missions.

Why: His tireless efforts to promote the work of missionary evangelists helped fund, build, and nurture numerous mission stations around the world.

Fifty-three

Who: Timothy Dwight (1752-1817)

What: Dwight, a distinguished Congregational minister and educator, was born in Northampton, Massachusetts. His mother was a daughter of Jonathan Edwards. He entered Yale College at the age of 13 and, graduating four years later, became a tutor; which position he resigned in 1777 to become chaplain in the Revolutionary army. He later became a pastor in Greenfield, Connecticut and, in 1795, was elected president of Yale College. He remained in this position until his death.

Why: His evangelical faith coupled with his prominent position at Yale influenced many young ministers during and after his lifetime.

Fifty-four

Who: Jonathan Edwards (1703-1758)

What: An important figure in American church history, Edwards was born in Connecticut to a renowned family of clergymen. He began reading Latin texts at the age of six and could read Greek and Hebrew by 13. He graduated from Yale in 1720 with highest honors. At about this time he also accepted Christ as his Savior. He served as a pastor for many years in Presbyterian and Congregational churches. His sermons during the revivals of the Great Awakening in 1734 through 1744 had a great impact. Among these was the famous "Sinners in the Hands of an Angry God." In 1757 he was elected president of Princeton College in New Jersey but died five weeks after his inauguration.

Why: He was a leading figure in New England Christianity and his books, like *Freedom of the Will*, did much to promote Reformed doctrines of original sin and predestination in colonial America.

Fifty-five

Who: Felicitas and Perpetua (d. 203)

What: Early Christian martyrs, the story of their death in the arena during the reign of Septimus Severus has been preserved in a document known as the "Diary of Perpetua."

Why: Their courage and faithful resolve as they faced death and the poignant tale of Felicitas giving birth in prison before her martyrdom (her child was placed with a Christian relative) is an incredible tale that has inspired many believers.

Fifty-six

Who: Charles Grandison Finney (1792-1875)

What: Finney, the great 19th century revivalist, abolitionist, and educator was born in Warren,

Connecticut but moved as a youth to New York and later New Jersey, where he went to school. His early career was as an attorney until he became interested in Bible study and began attending church services. Upon his conversion he gave up the practice of law and began preaching. He was ordained in the Presbyterian Church in 1824 and started holding the revival services that made him nationally famous. His unique methods became standard practices among revivalists and included his insistence that those who repented make an immediate decision for Christ and publicly proclaim their newfound faith. During his fruitful life he became a professor of theology and later president at Oberlin College in Ohio, he held revival services throughout the cities of the eastern United States and in England, he served as pastor of the Second Free Church of New York City and the Congregational Broadway Tabernacle, he was a staunch supporter of the abolishment of slavery, and he wrote a number of works including the influential *Lectures on Revival*.

Why: His preaching led to the conversion of an estimated half million people and his convictions about revival continue to influence evangelists.

Fifty-seven

Who: George Fox (1624-1691)

What: The founder of the Society of Friends or Quakers, Fox was born in Leicestershire, England, the son of a Puritan weaver. Finding little solace in the church, he decided at about the age of 22 to turn to God alone for spiritual companionship. He determined that organized religion was an enemy of true faith and that it led to formalism and hypocrisy. In 1647 he became an itinerant preacher and traveled widely across England and Scotland, as well as to Holland and America. He and his followers refused to take any oaths of allegiance or to serve in the military, decisions that often led to their imprisonment. He gained numerous converts to his beliefs, which included the assertions that professional clergy should be forbidden and that spiritual truth is gained only through the personal and immediate teaching of the Holy Spirit or "inner light."

Why: His mystical teachings have had a direct influence on a wide range of Christian writers and philosophers.

Fifty-eight

Who: Francis of Assisi (1182-1226)

What: The founder of the Franciscan order, Francesco Giovanni Bernardone was born in Assisi, Italy, the son of a wealthy cloth merchant. He lived a worldly and extravagant lifestyle as a young man until he joined the army and was captured. After his release he utterly embraced the Christian faith and abandoned his former life, much to the ire of his father. He became a strict ascetic and began working and ministering among a colony of lepers. In 1210 he drafted a set of rules for living and, along with a group of like-minded companions, he went to Rome to seek approval to start a monastic order. Innocent III gave them his blessing and they began to preach, care for the sick and poor, and launch mission trips to places like Egypt and Morocco. In 1222 his order was taken from him and given new rules. Despite his grief over these events, he humbly and characteristically submitted to the new authority and continued ministering until his death. He was canonized in 1228.

Why: His exemplary life of piety and his devotion to serving others was a model for the Franciscans and made them one of the most popular and influential orders in the Catholic Church.

Fifty-nine

Who: Frederick the Wise (1463-1525)

What: Born near Leipzeg, Germany, Frederick was Elector of Saxony during the height of the controversies surrounding Martin Luther. A pious man, he studied under Augustinian monks at Grimma, traveled to the Holy Land, and became a rapt student of the Bible under John von Staupitz. In 1502 he founded the University of Wittenberg, appointing Luther and Philip Melanchthon to professorships. Later, to protect Luther from the Catholic Church, he sent soldiers to accompany him during his trial and to later conceal him for his safety. While his original goal in the case of Luther was for justice to be served, he became increasingly convinced that the Reformer's doctrinal beliefs were correct. Prior to his death he joined the Protestant church.

Why: His protection of Luther allowed the great Reformer to not only work in relative peace, he was also protected from certain execution or assassination.

Sixty

Who: Charles E. Fuller (1887-1968)

What: A well known radio pioneer and educator, Fuller was born in Los Angeles and studied at Biola College. He was ordained in 1925 and became pastor of Calvary Church. He began a radio ministry in 1937 that could be heard on 600 CBS network stations. In 1947 he helped found Fuller Seminary.

Why: He was an early and successful advocate of using modern technology to bring the Gospel message to the masses.

Sixty-one

Who: Jonathan Goforth (1859-1936)

What: Goforth, a Canadian Presbyterian, studied at Knox College near his home in Western Ontario. While in school he began working among the inner city poor. After graduation he married Florence Bell-Smith and the two went to Honan, China, near the East China Sea, as missionaries. They later settled in Changteh in central China. Goforth's unique approach was to evangelize the educated and upper classes as well as the poor. Sadly their work in Changteh was cut short during the Boxer rebellion of 1900, an effort by Chinese nationalists to rid the country of Christian missionaries by murdering them and destroying their churches. The Goforths barely escaped with their lives. For a time they worked in safer regions of China and eventually were able to return to Changteh, where their efforts resulted in a regional revival. Goforth spent the last two years of his life traveling around Canada preaching and promoting the cause of missions.

Why: He remained in China after the Boxer uprising, unlike many missionaries, and was able to plant about 50 native evangelists in local churches.

Sixty-two

Who: Hugo Grotius (1583-1645)

What: A Dutch theologian and statesman, Grotius studied law under his father and, at the age of 23, became the advocate-general of Holland. His interests in theology led to his involvement with the controversies between the Calvinists and Arminians. He agreed with the latter group that men and women have the right to accept or refuse God's saving grace through Christ. At the Council of Dort in 1619 the Arminians were condemned and Grotius was sentenced to life in prison. He spent the next two years writing until his wife was able to help him escape. He fled to Paris and later moved to Sweden where he worked in the Swedish government. He died on a trip back to Holland when his ship wrecked.

Why: His historical and theological writings, particularly *On the Truth of the Christian Religion*, were very influential and widely studied.

Sixty-three

Who: Johann Gutenberg (c. 1400-1468)

What: The inventor of movable type and the father of printing is, ironically, a man of mystery with very little information about his life known for certain. He was born in Mainz, Germany and later his family moved to Strasbourg. In about 1438 he became a printer, returned to Mainz, and developed a partnership with a wealthy gold merchant named Johann Fust. They began a printing press and their first book, a Latin Bible known as the "Gutenberg Bible," was completed in about 1456. Around this same time Fust filed a lawsuit against Gutenberg to recover the money he had invested and Gutenberg was forced to relinquish his share of the business. He continued to dabble in various printing endeavors but died a pauper.

Why: His advances in printing technology allowed Bible translators to make the Scriptures available to the common person, a primary catalyst behind the success of the Reformation.

Sixty-four

Who: Frances Ridley Havergal (1836-1879)

What: Havergal was born in Worcestershire, England. "When fifteen years old," she once wrote, "I committed my soul to the Savior, and earth and heaven seemed brighter from that moment." Highly educated, her knowledge of Hebrew and Greek and modern languages was extensive and her hymn writing skills are celebrated to this day. About seventy-five of her hymns are in common use – including the classic "Take My Life and Let It Be."

Why: Her popularity and influence as an author and hymn writer have increased since her death.

Sixty-five

Who: Matthew Henry (1662-1714)

What: The renowned Bible commentator was born in Wales and was educated under the tutelage of his father, a Nonconformist minister. Henry began his career as a jurist but, in 1687, he was ordained a Presbyterian minister and he abandoned the practice of law. He served a church in Chester, England near Liverpool for nearly 25 years. During this time he wrote his multi-volume *Exposition of the Old and New Testaments*, later renamed *Matthew Henry's Commentaries*.

Why: His commentaries were unique and greatly influential in that they contained applicational and devotional material in addition to textual exposition.

Sixty-six

Who: John Hus (c. 1373-1415)

What: Born in Bohemia, or what is today the Czech Republic, Hus was of peasant stock but distinguished himself academically and was accepted into the University of Prague. In 1402 he was ordained to the priesthood and became the chaplain at the University. Although a loyal Roman Catholic he sympathized with the reform efforts of John Wycliffe in England. He became a leading figure in the region, writing and preaching on behalf of the religious rights of the people. For his convictions the church leadership excommunicated him. This only inspired him to further promote his reform views, which now included disputing such matters as worship of the saints, transubstantiation, and the primacy of human authority over the Scriptures. In 1414 he was summoned before the Council of Constance and in 1415, despite promises from the pope that he would not be condemned and executed, he was burned at the stake.

Why: His popularity made him a martyr to the people of Bohemia and his death helped lay the groundwork for the acceptance of future reformers.

Sixty-seven

Who: Irenaeus (c. 2nd century)

What: Born somewhere in western Asia Minor, probably Smyrna, Irenaeus studied religion and philosophy under Polycarp, the bishop of Smyrna. He was a missionary to Gaul, or modern day France, and eventually became the bishop of Lyons when the previous bishop was martyred during the reign of Marcus Aurelius. He served with great distinction and there are indications that most of the population of Lyons accepted the message of Christ during his lifetime. He wrote extensively, including his best-known treatise, *Against All Heresies*, which defended the true faith against Gnosticism.

Why: He was the first early church Father to extensively use the entire New Testament in his writings and to show the unity between the Old and New Testaments.

Sixty-eight

Who: Henry Allan ("Harry") Ironside (1878-1951)

What: Born in Toronto, Canada, Ironside moved with his family in 1886 to Los Angeles and there accepted Christ at the age of 14. He joined the Salvation Army and began preaching at their gatherings and rallies. He became nationally known as the "Boy Preacher of Los Angeles." In 1896 he joined the Plymouth Brethren and spent nearly 35 years speaking at Bible conferences in the United States and Canada. In 1930 he became the pastor of Moody Memorial Church in Chicago. Here he began a radio ministry that was broadcast on the Moody radio network. He died in New Zealand while on an evangelistic crusade and was buried there.

Why: He was a well known and trusted Bible commentator and preacher whose books were among the best-selling inspirational works of his day.

Sixty-nine

Who: Jerome (c. 345-420)

What: Born in Dalmatia, or modern day Croatia, of Christian parents, Jerome went to Rome at the age of 12 to study Latin and Greek. He became a Christian at 19 and decided to move to Antioch. Here he lived in a cave and spent his time studying the Scriptures and learning Hebrew from a local rabbi. In 382 Pope Damasus called him to Rome to become a papal secretary and to undertake a new translation of the

Hebrew and Greek Scriptures. He completed the work many years later from a monastery he oversaw in Bethlehem.

Why: His translation, known as the Latin Vulgate, became the official and authorized source text for the Roman Catholic Church.

Seventy

Who: Adoniram Judson (1788-1850)

What: Born near Malden, Massachusetts Judson was the son of a Congregational minister. He graduated from Brown University and studied for a time at Andover Theological Seminary. In 1810 he was licensed to preach in the Congregational church and joined with several others to petition the General Association of Ministers for a missionary commission to China. He was sent to England to secure the cooperation of the London Missionary Society but failed to gain their approval. He returned to America where the American Board of Commissioners for Foreign Missions, a Congregational association, sent him to India in 1812. Accompanied by his wife, Anne, Judson arrived in Calcutta but soon got into trouble with the Board after his views on baptism changed to the conviction that full immersion was necessary. He joined the Baptist church and the couple moved to Burma where they lived in the English Baptist mission home. He began an earnest study of the Burmese language, although it took him nearly six years to gain the necessary linguistic skills to preach in the native tongue. It was another six years before he led the first person to Christ. In 1824 the Anglo-Burmese war broke out and Judson was imprisoned for two years. Shortly after his release Anne died. Judson continued his work and in 1833 he completed a translation of the Bible into Burmese. During this time he married Sarah Hall Boardman, returning to America in 1845 due to her failing health. Sadly she died on the voyage. He went back to Burma in 1846 and spent the rest of his life working on a Burmese dictionary. Like his second wife, he also died at sea while sailing to Martinique where he hoped to recuperate from an illness.

Why: He is considered by historians as the greatest American missionary.

Seventy-one

Who: Justin Martyr (c. 100-165)

What: Born in Samaria, Justin was well educated and grew up in a family of means who allowed him to travel extensively. He earnestly sought the truth in various religions and philosophies but didn't find peace until an elderly believer led him to Christ. He became an itinerant minister and traveled from city to city preaching the Gospel. He was captured in Rome during a visit and was beheaded along with several other Christians.

Why: His book *First Apology* affirmed to believers and nonbelievers alike the superiority of Christianity over other religions.

Seventy-two

Who: John Keble (1792-1866)

What: Keble graduated from Oxford in 1810 and was ordained in 1815. In 1827 he published his well-known

volume, *The Christian Year*; ninety-six editions of which appeared before his death. A sermon preached by him on "National Apostacy" is regarded as the origin of the Tractarian movement in 1833. He wrote eight of the "Tracts for the Times." He was the author of several volumes of hymns including *A Metrical Version of the Psalms*, 1839, and *Lyra Innocentium*, 1846.
Why: His sermons and writings on the proper relationship between the church and the state had a great influence on Christians in England and the United States in the 19th century.

Seventy-three

Who: Soren Aaby Kierkegaard (1813-1855)
What: Born in Copenhagen, Kierkegaard exhibited from an early age the depression and insecurity that would plague him his entire life. He studied theology at the University of Copenhagen, graduating in 1840, but was never ordained. Most of his life was spent writing works that stressed the necessity of a moral life and the "otherness" of God. His best known work,

Either-Or, was an anonymously published debate between ethical and aesthetic ideas. In his last years he wrote works that argued against the theology and practice of the Danish state church on the grounds that religion is for the individual soul and is to be separated absolutely from the state and the world.

Why: He was an early existential philosopher and his writing greatly influenced the Neo-orthodox theologians of the early 20th century.

Seventy-four

Who: Martin Luther King, Jr. (1929-1968)

What: The great civil rights leader was born in Atlanta, Georgia and studied at Morehouse College, Crozer Theological Seminary, and Boston University. In 1954 he became a pastor in Montgomery, Alabama at the Dexter Avenue Baptist Church. He was later co-pastor with his father of the Ebenezer Baptist Church in Atlanta, a church founded by his grandfather. In Montgomery in 1955, Rosa Parks, a respected member of the local NAACP, was arrested after refusing to give up her seat on a bus to a white passenger. This event followed years of mistreatment by bus drivers who had forced black riders to sit in the backs of buses. King was chosen to head the Montgomery Improvement Association, which had organized a boycott to protest the unfair practices of the bus companies. After more than a year of peaceful protests and savage attacks from white segregationists, the Supreme Court upheld a previous Federal ruling and desegregated the bus lines. King's national stature rose and in 1957 he helped found the Southern Christian Leadership Conference (SCLC). Jailed and threatened many times, King and his followers worked tirelessly to end racial discrimination. Among his many famous speeches was the "I Have a Dream" message he gave at a massive protest in Washington, D.C. in 1963. Here he shared his hopes for the civil rights movement and how it would improve the lives of all Americans. His efforts earned the Nobel Peace Prize in 1964. Sadly, as he often predicted, he was assassinated in 1968 in Memphis.

Why: He applied Christian principles of non-violence to a movement that changed the social landscape of the United States.

Seventy-five

Who: John Knox (c. 1514-1572)

What: Born in Haddington, Scotland and educated at the University of Glasgow, Knox was originally a Roman Catholic priest. In 1543 he converted to Protestantism due, primarily, to the preaching of the reformer George Wishart. Although Wishart was eventually executed for heresy, Knox continued preaching until his capture by the French in 1547 when they attacked Saint Andrews. He was forced to labor in a French galley for almost two years until Edward VI, the king of England, secured his release. He moved to England and became the royal chaplain in 1551. When Catholic Queen Mary took the throne in 1553 he fled to Frankfurt and later to Geneva. Here he met Calvin and began studying his doctrines. He preached widely throughout Europe for a number of years until his return to Scotland in 1559. He denounced the Catholic Church and Scotland's Catholic regent, Mary of Guise. He supported the Protestant revolt against the regency, a hopeless cause until England's Elizabeth I, who had succeeded her half-sister Mary, agreed to support them. After the death of Mary of Guise, the Protestants took control of the Scottish government and Knox's Confession of Faith was adopted by the Parliament. Control was lost briefly upon the return of yet another Catholic Mary, Mary Stuart, who reigned from 1560 to 1567. She had Knox arrested for treason, although he was later acquitted. He spent his remaining years after Mary's death preaching and writing.

Why: He was the father of the Scottish Reformation and the architect of various branches of the Presbyterian and Reformed churches that exist today.

Seventy-six

Who: Hugh Latimer (c. 1485-1555)

What: An English bishop and martyr, Latimer was born in Leicestershire, England and received his education at Christ's College, Cambridge. In 1530 he was appointed a royal chaplain and in 1535 he became the bishop of Worcester. His sermons calling for church reform led to his arrest, although Edward VI later freed him. When Mary Tudor became queen he was condemned for heresy and burned at the stake along with fellow reformer Nicholas Ridley.

Why: His popularity and courage helped embolden Protestant believers during the reign of Mary.

Seventy-seven

Who: Clive Staples (C. S.) Lewis (1898-1963)

What: Born in Belfast, Ireland and educated at Oxford, Lewis was a professor of medieval and Renaissance literature at Cambridge. He described his conversion to Christianity from atheism in the 1955 book *Surprised by Joy*. He was a lecturer on ethical and religious matters on the BBC and wrote numerous influential books including *Mere Christianity*, *The*

Screwtape Letters, and the children's classics *The Chronicles of Narnia*.

Why: He influenced many people to become Christians who might not have considered the faith otherwise, especially college students.

Seventy-eight

Who: David Livingstone (1813-1873)

What: A renowned missionary and explorer, Livingstone grew up in Glasgow, Scotland in a poor family. He studied on his own and was able to enter the University of Glasgow in 1830 where he earned degrees in theology and medicine. His desire was to become a missionary to China; however, due to the dangerous conditions in that country at the time, the London Missionary Society sent him to Africa in 1840. He began at the missionary station of Robert Moffat in South Africa, whose daughter he later married, and began pushing steadily northward, building stations along the way. Believing that exploration and missions went hand in hand, he became a renowned explorer, discovering Lake N'gami in 1849 and Victoria Falls in 1853. He sent his family home to England and continued his trek deeper into uncharted territory, traveling nearly 1,400 miles on foot and by boat and preaching the Gospel along the way. He went to England in 1856 where he was hailed as a national hero. When he returned to Africa a year later he had resigned from the Mission Society and worked directly for the British government. His goals were national, ethical, and spiritual: to find the source of the Nile, to end the slave trade, and to share the message of Christ. He was lost for a time from the world, which led to a search in 1870 by journalist Henry Stanley, whose line upon discovering him "Dr. Livingstone, I presume?" has become famous. He died three years later, found on his knees in the position of prayer by his native guides.

Why: He opened the African frontier to missions and his diligent efforts to end the slave trade were largely successful.

Seventy-nine

Who: Martin Luther (1483-1546)

What: Luther, the hero of the Reformation, was born in the village of Eisleben. He entered the University at Erfurt in 1501 and graduated with honors. In 1505 he entered an Augustinian monastery at Erfurt and was consecrated to the priesthood in 1507. He was a diligent scholar and in 1508 was called to the chair of Philosophy at the University of Wittenberg. In 1512 he received the degree of Doctor of Theology. In the meantime he made a pilgrimage to Rome where he saw much corruption among the clergy; but still his faith was strong in the Roman Church. It was the shameless sale of indulgences by Tetzel, authorized by Leo X, which first opened his eyes and determined him to make public opposition. On October 31, 1517, at midday, Luther posted his ninety-five Theses against the Merits of Indulgences on the church door at Wittenberg. The burning of the pope's bull of excommunication in 1520, the Diet of Worms in 1521, Luther's concealment in the castle at Wartburg, and his marriage to a former nun in 1525 are just a few events in his epic life. It was during his Wartburg captivity that he translated the New Testament, published in 1522, into the mother tongue of the German people.

Why: He is one of the giants of the Christian faith and was, in large part, both the inspiration and the impetus behind the Reformation.

Eighty

Who: John Gresham Machen (1881-1937)

What: Born in Baltimore, Machen was a tremendous scholar who studied at Johns Hopkins and Princeton in the United States and at Marburg in Germany. Ordained in 1914 he became a professor of New Testament literature at Princeton Theological Seminary. He left the school due to his conservative theology and the school's rapid drift toward liberalism. In 1929 he founded the Westminster Theological Seminary and became its president and professor of New Testament. He took similar steps when he resigned from the

Presbyterian Board of Missions to found an independent society and when he and a group of like-minded clergy started the Orthodox Presbyterian church.

Why: He was a staunch defender of conservative Christianity at a time when scholars of his stature were nearly all liberal.

Eighty-one

Who: Asa Mahan (1800-1889)

What: Born in Vernon, New York, Mahan studied at Andover Theological Seminary and became a pastor at churches in New York and Ohio. For 15 years, beginning in 1835, he served as president of Oberlin College. Here he established that degrees would be granted to women and minorities under the same conditions and terms as men, a radical directive for that time. In 1871 he retired to England where he preached and wrote until his death.

Why: He was a staunch abolitionist and an advocate for women, expressing in his books and sermons that

to deny the rights of equality was to deny a central
tenet of Christianity.

Eighty-two

Who: Peter Marshall (1902-1949)

What: Born in Scotland, Marshall came to the United
States in 1927 to study religion at Columbia
Theological Seminary in Decatur, Georgia. He became
a naturalized citizen and began preaching in
Presbyterian churches in Georgia and Washington,
D.C. In 1947 he became the Chaplain of the United
States Senate, a position he held until his premature
death from a heart attack at the age of 47. His most
popular book was *Mr. Jones, Meet the Master*.

Why: He redefined the role of Senate chaplain, despite
the brevity of his tenure, and became an influential
minister to those who governed the nation during the
critical years after World War II.

Eighty-three

Who: Henry Martyn (1781-1812)

What: An English missionary to India, Martyn was inspired by the work and writings of William Carey and David Brainerd. In 1803 he was ordained a deacon in the Church of England and two years later obtained a chaplaincy from the East India Company. Stationed in Calcutta he studied the local dialects so that he could preach and translate the New Testament. His frail health forced him to leave India in 1810 and he sailed for Persia, hoping that a change in climate would improve his condition. He ministered to the Muslims, once again preaching on the streets and translating the Scriptures. He died of tuberculosis while on a mission trip to Turkey.

Why: He was the first missionary to both the Hindus and the Muslims and his *Journals*, where he detailed the great importance of missions, inspired many in the 19th century to spread the Gospel around the world.

Eighty-four

Who: Philipp Melanchthon (1497-1560)

What: A German Reformer, Melancthon studied Greek at the University of Heidelberg before taking a teaching position in Greek studies at the University of Wittenberg. Here he met Martin Luther and the two became close allies and like-minded associates. Melancthon is often called the organizational genius behind the German Reformation. He wrote the Augsburg Confession and assumed Luther's mantle of leadership after the great Reformer's death. Melancthon's personality was quite different from Luther's, however, and his tendency to seek compromise rather than stand firm on certain key issues resulted in an early schism in the Lutheran church.

Why: His great intellect produced many of the early, official writings of the Lutheran church and he was the developer of the German system of education that continues to influence the schooling of children in that nation.

Eighty-five

Who: John Milton (1608-1674)

What: One of the greatest English poets, Milton was born in London and was educated at Cambridge. His family's wealth allowed him to travel extensively after graduation and to spend six years at his father's estate writing poetry. He wrote a number of pamphlets that defended the Presbyterian system of government against the Episcopal practices of the Anglican Church. In 1652 he became totally blind – a condition that did not keep him from writing such works as the epic "Paradise Lost." He also wrote 19 versions of various Psalms, which appeared in his *Poems in English and Latin*, 1673.

Why: He represents the best influences of both the Protestant Reformation and the Renaissance.

Eighty-six

Who: Robert Moffat (1795-1883)

What: A Scottish Congregationalist missionary to Africa, Moffat was born to a poor family and spent his early years working as an estate gardener. In 1814 he sought a commission from the London Missionary Society and was sent within a year to South Africa. He settled in Cape Town and in 1819 married Mary

Smith (1795-1870), the daughter of a former employer. In 1820 the couple left Cape Town and settled among the tribes west of the Vaal River. Here he translated the entire Bible and *Pilgrim's Progress* into the native language. He was a great influence on his son-in-law, David Livingstone, and encouraged him in his desire to take the Gospel deeper into uncharted Africa. He retired to England after the death of his wife and spent the rest of his life writing and preaching.

Why: He laid the foundation for the success of subsequent mission work in southern and central Africa and persevered in his work despite many setbacks.

Eighty-seven

Who: Dwight Lyman Moody (1837-1899)

What: One of the great 19th century American evangelists, Moody was born in East Northfield, Massachusetts to a family of modest means. His father died when Moody was four and financial circumstances and his own unruly nature kept him from receiving more than a superficial education. In 1854 he became a shoe clerk in Boston. A year later his life changed forever when his Sunday school teacher, Edward Kimball, led him to Christ. In 1856 he went to Chicago and started a successful business selling shoes. He joined the Plymouth Congregational Church and was charged with starting a Sunday school program. He embraced this task with great vigor and before long the church was offering classes to over 1,500 students. In 1860 he gave up his business and devoted himself full-time to city missionary work. He was prominent in raising money for various Christian ministries and in 1865 he was made president of the Chicago Young Men's Christian Association. Although not formally trained, Moody was a gifted speaker and evangelist and by 1871 he had erected a large church on LaSalle Street, near the site of the current Moody Memorial Church. Ira David Sankey joined him in Chicago and helped him further his evangelistic efforts with hymn singing. In a series of notable revival meetings in England and America they became a famous evangelistic team, establishing a model for future evangelists like Billy

Sunday and Billy Graham. An advocate of education, perhaps because of his own childhood, Moody opened the Northfield seminary for young women in 1879 in Northfield, Massachusetts and, in 1881, the adjacent Mount Hermon School for boys. In 1889 he established in Chicago the first Bible school of its kind in the country, the Chicago Evangelization Society. Renamed later the Moody Bible Institute, it trained Christian workers in Bible study and in practical methods of social reform. He founded the Colportage Association in 1895 to produce Christian literature at a modest price for mass distribution. He died during a crusade in Kansas City.

Why: He led millions to Christ through his various and far-flung evangelistic activities and his educational and publishing institutions continue to impact the lives of people around the world.

Eighty-eight

Who: Hannah More (1745-1833)

What: Born near Bristol, England More was educated at a school run by her older sisters. She began writing at an early age and by the time she was in her mid-thirties she had published a number of dramas and works of religious fiction. She began writing tracts during the time of the French Revolution, primarily to promote the Christian faith against the agnostic philosophies that were becoming influential. Her tracts were tremendously popular and led to the creation of the Religious Tract Society. Her social views, particularly regarding the plight of poor women and children and the evils of slavery, were influenced by preachers and reform advocates like William Wilberforce and John Newton. She used her wealth to establish schools, press the government for social improvements, and set up relief agencies.

Why: Her books, poems, and tracts were very popular and her social activism helped improve the lives of the helpless and oppressed.

Eighty-nine

Who: George Campbell Morgan (1863-1945)

What: Born in Gloucestershire, England, Morgan was ordained in the Congregational Church and began his ministry at churches in Birmingham and London. In 1883 he began working with Dwight L. Moody and Ira Sankey during a revival in Britain. He went with them to the United States in 1896 and spent several years in America as an evangelist and Bible conference speaker. He returned to England in 1904 and served Westminster Congregational Chapel in London for 13 years, building it from a small church into one of the largest and most influential congregations in England. He traveled widely for the next 15 years, conducting numerous evangelistic crusades in America and Canada. For a time he was the pastor of Tabernacle Presbyterian Church in Philadelphia. In 1935 he returned Westminster where he remained until shortly before his death. He was the author of many Bible commentaries and edited the *Westminster Pulpit*.

Why: His collections of sermons and Bible studies were widely popular and highly influential during the first half of the 20th century.

Ninety

Who: Robert Morrison (1782-1834)

What: The first Protestant missionary to China, Morrison began studying Chinese along with theology and medicine as a student in Northumbria, England. In 1807 the London Missionary Society sent him to Canton, China. He spent his early years on the mission field in near seclusion as he attempted to master the language. His proficiency grew to the point that he became an interpreter for the British East India Company. He worked on a number of printed translations including a collection of hymns, prayers from the Book of Common Prayer, and, eventually, a translation of the entire Bible – a mammoth project he completed in 1823. He went to England for a short time in 1824 but returned to China within two years where he spent the remainder of his life.

Why: He saw very few converts during his lifetime but his translation work and the establishment of a mission school laid a solid foundation for the missionaries who followed him.

Ninety-one

Who: George Müller (1805-1898)

What: An English preacher and renowned advocate of the power of prayer, Müller was born in Germany but later became a naturalized British subject. Educated in Germany, he went to London in 1828 to seek a commission from a missionary organization. In 1830, however, he gave up the idea of missionary work and became the minister of a small congregation in Devonshire. He believed that the temporal as well as the spiritual needs of life could be supplied entirely by prayer, and on this principle he refused to take a fixed salary. After two years here, Müller moved to Bristol where he spent the rest of his life. He devoted himself particularly to the care of orphan children. He began by taking a few into his care, but soon their number increased to over 2,000. He built five large houses at Ashley Down, near Bristol. The money required for building and maintaining the orphanage was voluntarily contributed. When he was over seventy he and his wife started on a preaching mission that lasted nearly

17 years and included Europe, America, India, Australia, and China. Together they traveled over two hundred thousand miles and preached to more than three million people. When Müller died his possessions were valued at less than a thousand pounds although he had handled millions during his lifetime – all secured solely through faith and prayer.

Why: His triumphant life, recounted in his widely circulated book *The Narration of Some of the Lord's Dealings with George Müller*, was a testimony to the power of prayer and inspired many Christians to undertake great causes on faith alone.

Ninety-two

Who: Andrew Murray (1828-1917)

What: Born in South Africa, Murray was educated in Aberdeen, Scotland where he lived with an uncle. In 1828 he was ordained in the Dutch Reformed Church and returned to his native land. He was appointed to a church in the Orange River Sovereignty but traveled widely throughout the region, preaching to thousands who otherwise had no pastor. When revival broke out in America and Britain, he was serving a large congregation in Worcester, South Africa. Murray and his congregation were greatly affected by these events and the church became actively involved in spreading the revival throughout their country. Among his many other accomplishments, Murray founded a seminary, a missionary training school, and the first Y.M.C.A. in South Africa; he conducted extensive evangelistic crusades in North America, Europe, and South Africa; and he wrote a number of influential books, including the classic *With Christ in the School of Prayer*.

Why: He was an influential and world famous evangelist and preacher during the late 19th and early 20th centuries and his devotional writings, for which he is best known today, were eagerly read by millions.

Ninety-three

Who: John Henry Newman (1801-1890)

What: Newman, a cardinal in the Roman Catholic Church, was born in London and graduated from

Oxford in 1820. For several years he was a tutor at that college. He was a leader of the High Church party in the Church of England and had great influence among the young men at Oxford. He was ordained to the ministry in the Church of England in 1824 but in 1845 joined the Catholic Church. He was the most prominent and influential English Roman Catholic of the 19th century. His collected works include many volumes on doctrinal and ecclesiastical subjects as well as translations of Latin hymns.

Why: He greatly influenced the English Roman Catholic and High Anglican churches of the late 19th and early 20th centuries.

Ninety-four

Who: John Newton (1725-1807)

What: Newton, the author of the hymn "Amazing Grace," was born in London, the son of a pious mother who died when he was only seven years of age. His only "schooling" was from his eighth to his tenth year. He was engaged in the African slave trade for several years, and was even himself held as a slave at one time in Sierra Leone. He bragged of his sinful nature, but was converted in a storm at sea while returning from Africa. He married a devout Christian in 1750 and became a minister in the Established Church in 1758, preaching at a church in Olney, near Cambridge. He remained here for nearly sixteen years, becoming friends with the poet William Cowper, who was joint author with him of the *Olney Hymns*, 1779. Soon after the appearance of this volume he moved to London where he was rector of St. Mary Woolnoth. Newton wrote his own epitaph, which included the following: John Newton, once an infidel and libertine, was, by the rich mercy of our Lord and Saviour Jesus Christ, preserved, restored, and pardoned, and appointed to preach the Faith he had long labored to destroy.

Why: He was an influential minister in his time but his hymn "Amazing Grace" has had lasting influence on believers and nonbelievers alike to this day.

Ninety-five

Who: Florence Nightingale (1820-1910)

What: Born into a wealthy English family, Nightingale believed that God had called her to abandon her life of luxury to serve others. She received a classical education focused on the humanities but developed an early interest in medicine when she saw the deplorable conditions in many of the English hospitals. She decided to become a nurse and when war broke out between Russia and England in 1854 she went to Crimea to volunteer her services, taking 38 nurses with her. Before she arrived the death rate in the filthy hospitals, which crawled with vermin and disease, was nearly fifty percent. Her valiant efforts to make the facilities clean and the environment conducive to healing resulted in a death rate of less than five percent. The stories of her courage on the battlefront, the successes she achieved as a care provider, the difficulties she had with inept and jealous doctors, and the Crimean fever that nearly killed her made her an international heroine. Nicknamed "the Lady with the Lamp" for her habit of checking on soldiers late into the night, her popularity inspired health care changes around the world. Thousands sent her contributions to help with her work, money she used to build a school for nurses at King's College after the war. Although an invalid during the last forty years of her life, she wrote extensively about nursing and was a tireless champion for hospital reform.

Why: She was a world-renowned figure whose selfless life influenced the work of many Christian social activists.

Ninety-six

Who: Patrick (c. 389- c. 461)

What: The famous Celtic missionary to Ireland, Patrick (or, more correctly, Patricius) was captured at the age of 16 by pirates and was sold into slavery to sheepherders in Northern Ireland. After six years he escaped and made his way to Gaul (or modern day France) where he entered a monastery. He returned to England but had a vision where he saw the people of Ireland calling to him, asking that he minister to them. In about 432 he answered this call and began preaching throughout the Irish countryside, converting large numbers of people from both the peasant and the noble classes. He built dozens of churches, which led to the conversion and baptism of thousands.

Why: His efforts not only transformed the religious landscape of Ireland, he greatly influenced the work of missionaries in Britain and on the European continent as well.

Ninety-seven

Who: Edward Perronet (1726-1792)

What: Perronet, an Independent English clergyman, was the son of Vincent Perronet, vicar of Shoreham, who was a friend and supporter of the Wesleys. Edward was educated in the Church of England but became a Wesleyan preacher. In 1756 the question arose among the Methodists concerning separation from the Church of England. The Wesleys strenuously opposed this move; Perronet just as strongly favored and urged it. He later joined the Independent or Dissenting Church, where he remained until his death. He is the author of the beloved hymn "All Hail the Power of Jesus' Name."

Why: His convictions helped to give further distinction between the Methodist and Anglican churches.

Ninety-eight

Who: Polycarp (c. 69-c . 155)

What: An early church father, Polycarp was a disciple to the apostle John. A link between those who had witnessed the life and teachings of Christ and the 2nd century church, his writings take on special meaning when he refers to New Testament events and to Pauline letters. He was arrested during the persecution of Antoninus Pius and, after refusing to recant his faith, was burned at the stake.

Why: His writings and faithfulness were a source of authenticity and encouragement to early believers.

Ninety-nine

Who: Luther Rice (1783-1836)

What: Born in Northbor, Massachusetts, Rice studied at Williams College and Andover Theological Seminary. He became interested in missions and, along with Adoniram Judson, founded the American Board of Commissioners for Foreign Missions in 1810. In 1812 he went to India, leaving port a Congregational minister but arriving as a Baptist – a conversion that took place during the long journey through the influence of Baptist missionaries who were also on board. He returned to America after a year to help raise funds for other missionaries. He organized the General Convention of the Baptist Denomination in the United States for Foreign Missions in 1814, which sent many missionaries around the world. In 1822 he helped found Columbian University (later renamed George Washington University) in Washington, D.C., from where he published the Baptist weekly, *The Columbian Star*. Despite suffering a stroke in 1832 he continued pressing for the support of missions until his death.

Why: His fruitful life supported thousands of missionaries and produced numerous schools and mission organizations.

One hundred

Who: Horatio G. Spafford (1828-1888)

What: Spafford was a wealthy Chicago businessman who lost his fortune during the Chicago fire. Despite this, he and his wife, Anna, devoted countless hours to helping the survivors. Later he sent Anna and his four daughters to England for a rest. While crossing the Atlantic their ship sank in a collision. Anna survived and sent him the heartbreaking telegram, "Saved Alone." Several weeks later, as Spafford's own ship passed near the spot where his daughters died, he wrote the hymn "It Is Well With My Soul." In 1881 the Spaffords moved to Jerusalem – taking two daughters born after the shipwreck – and helped found a group called the American Colony. Its mission was to serve the poor. The colony later became the subject of the Nobel prize-winning novel *Jerusalem*. Few hymn stories are as powerful as this one.

Why: His unwavering faith has comforted countless grieving Christians; helping to assure them that God is in control, regardless of the circumstances.

One hundred one

Who: Earl of Shaftesbury, Anthony Ashley Cooper (Lord Ashley) (1801-1885)

What: Born in London and educated at Oxford, he entered Parliament in 1826 as a member of the conservative party. A devout Christian he used his status to undertake a series of social reforms and pushed through laws designed to protect those with mental illness, provide improved housing conditions for the poor, and eliminate the exploitation of children in factories and as chimney sweeps. He developed and oversaw a number of ministry organizations including the Society for the Prevention of Cruelty to Children, the British and Foreign Bible Society, the Pastoral Aid Society, and the London City Mission.

Why: He was largely responsible for the passage of many laws that protected the most vulnerable members of English society and his example inspired many Christian social activists and humanitarians in America.

One hundred two

Who: Charles Haddon Spurgeon (1834-1892)

What: Born in London, Spurgeon was the son of a Congregational minister. He joined the Baptist church in 1850 after his conversion and began preaching immediately. Demonstrating powerful skills as an orator he filled the small chapels he spoke in to capacity. In the 1850s, while a vast new church was being built for him, he preached to audiences approaching 10,000 people at the Surrey Music Hall. When the Metropolitan Tabernacle was completed in 1861 it held over 6,000 and could be used for numerous church related and mission outreach functions, a new concept in that day. Among his many accomplishments was the creation of a monthly magazine, *The Sword and Trowel*; the publication of over 2,000 sermons and

numerous books, including *Commenting and Commentaries*; the establishment of the Stockwell Orphanage, which housed 500 children; the creation of the Colportage Society to distribute books, tracts, and Bibles; and the establishment of a pastor's college.
Why: He was the most influential British preacher and evangelist of the 19th century.

One hundred three

Who: Harriet Beecher Stowe (1811-1896)

What: Stowe, the daughter of the famous preacher Lyman Beecher, was born in Litchfield, Connecticut in 1812. Her father became President of Lane Theological Seminary, Cincinnati, Ohio, in 1832; and in 1833 she was married to Calvin E. Stowe, a professor in the seminary. Her book *Uncle Tom's Cabin*, which was first published in 1852 as a serial in the *National Era* magazine and later in book form, is one of the most widely known and historic volumes in the entire range of American literature. It is a work of fiction that, by means of the pathetic picture that it draws of the ills of slave life and the cruelties involved in slave ownership, did much to precipitate the American Civil War (1861-1865). Mrs. Stowe published more than forty volumes in all, many of them being works of fiction. Her *Religious Poems* appeared in 1867.

Why: Her book about the evils of slavery, *Uncle Tom's Cabin*, is credited with raising the passions that ignited the American Civil War.

One hundred four

Who: James Strong (1822-1894)

What: Born in New York City, Strong studied ancient languages at Wesleyan University. A man of many talents he worked as a college professor, the president of a railroad company, and as a city administrator. In 1868 he became professor of exegetical theology at Drew Theological Seminary where he remained until shortly before his death. Among his numerous books was the seminal *Exhaustive Concordance of the Bible*.

Why: He was a great defender of conservative theology and biblical interpretation and his concordance remains a standard for many evangelical Christians.

One hundred five

Who: Charles T. Studd (1862-1931)

What: A national sports hero in England and a renowned cricket player, Studd abandoned fame and fortune after his conversion at a Moody-Sankey evangelistic crusade. He gave away over 100,000 pounds and went to China in 1885 to serve under Hudson Taylor at the Inland China Mission. He married an Irish missionary and the two worked together until ill health forced them to return to England in 1894. They traveled in America for a time – where Studd ministered on various university campuses – until he received a call in 1900 to work as a missionary in South India. After another brief return to England in 1906 he decided to undertake a mission campaign in Central Africa. Eventually his wife, daughters, and two sons-in-law joined him and together they founded the

Worldwide Evangelization Crusade. He remained in Africa until his death.

Why: He is a wonderful example of someone who abandoned the temporal pleasures of this world in favor of eternal riches in heaven.

One hundred six

Who: William Ashley (Billy) Sunday (1862-1935)

What: Born in Ames, Iowa Sunday grew up in an army orphanage after the death of his father, a Union soldier. For eight years, beginning in 1883, he was a renowned baseball player for various National League teams. He became a Christian after listening to a street preacher in Chicago and immediately abandoned his baseball career, where he was making $5,000 per year, for a job in the Y.M.C.A. that paid less than $100 a month. After working as a chaplain during World War I he returned home and began holding evangelistic crusades. Known for his physically exuberant and theatrical preaching, he became very popular and attracted thousands to his tent meetings. It is estimated that several hundred thousand people came to Christ during his crusades.

Why: His conservative views were very influential among evangelical churches during the early 20th century.

One hundred seven

Who: James Hudson Taylor (1832-1905)

What: Born in Yorkshire, England, Taylor went to China in 1854, after studying medicine and theology, to become a missionary with the China Evangelization Society. He adopted the then unique custom of wearing only Chinese clothing so as to assimilate better into the local culture. In 1860 he returned to England to begin translating the New Testament into the Ningpo dialect. After completing this project in 1866, he returned to China with his wife, children, and a group of other missionaries as founding members of the newly formed China Inland Mission (CIM). By the time of his death there were more than 200 CIM stations throughout China.

Why: His belief that missionaries should dress and live like the people they are trying to reach continues to influence mission efforts to this day.

One hundred eight

Who: Gerhard Tersteegen (1697-1769)

What: Tersteegen, a pious mystic of the eighteenth century, was born in Mörs, Germany. He was apprenticed as a young man to his older brother, a shopkeeper. He purchased a humble cottage near Mühlheim, where he led a life of seclusion and self-denial for many years. At about 30 years of age he began to preach in private and public gatherings. His influence became very great; such was his reputation for piety and his success in talking, preaching, and writing about spiritual matters. He wrote 111 hymns, most of which appeared in his *Spiritual Flower Garden*, 1731.

Why: His pious life influenced many in his day and some of his hymns, like "Lo, God is Here," can still be found in many hymnals.

One hundred nine

Who: Quintus Septimius Florens Tertullian (c. 160-c. 220)

What: Born in Carthage, North Africa, Tertullian studied law as a young man. In about 195 he converted to Christianity and spent the rest of his life utilizing his skills as a rhetorician to defend the faith against pagan philosophies and heresies. He wrote various influential apologies, including *Against Marcion* where he condemned one of the key advocates of Gnosticism.

Why: He was an early codifier of Christian doctrine and held influential views on matters of infant baptism, moral purity, and Trinitarian doctrine.

One hundred ten

Who: Augustus Montague Toplady (1740-1778)

What: Born in Surrey, England to an affluent family Toplady visited Ireland at the age of 16 and converted to Christianity at a service held in a barn – an experience he considered both ironic and providential since he had felt no spiritual yearnings at the grand cathedral his family attended. He was ordained to the ministry in the Church of England in 1762 and in 1768 he became vicar of Broadhembury, a position he held until his death. An advocate of Calvinism he came into frequent conflict with John Wesley. His volume of *Psalms and Hymns for Public and Private Worship* was published in 1776 and included the classic "Rock of Ages."

Why: He attained great influence in his brief life and many of his hymns are sung to this day.

One hundred eleven

Who: Reuben Archer (R. A.) Torrey (1856-1928)

What: A renowned Congregational evangelist and author, Torrey was born in Hoboken, New Jersey and studied at Yale University. After serving briefly as a pastor in Ohio he moved to Germany to study at Leipzig. In 1889, Dwight L. Moody asked him direct his new Bible institute, later named after its founder, and to fill the role of senior pastor at the Chicago Avenue Church, now the Moody Memorial Church. He remained here for 12 years, helping to build both into thriving and influential institutions. He performed the identical task in Los Angeles where he was dean at the Bible Institute of Los Angeles and pastor of Church of the Open Door. During his lifetime he conducted numerous worldwide evangelistic crusades and was a frequent Bible conference speaker. He wrote more than 40 books.

Why: His impact on two major Bible colleges and churches, his many speaking engagements, and his popular books helped define and develop the evangelical church during the early 20th century.

One hundred twelve

Who: William Tyndale (c. 1494-1536)

What: Although the exact location of his birth is unknown, Tyndale attended both Oxford and Cambridge where he excelled as a Greek scholar. Inspired by the efforts of Martin Luther to make the Bible available in a German translation, Tyndale decided to do the same for English speaking Christians. He went to Germany to study Hebrew under Jewish scholars and while there translated and published a New Testament in 1525. It was smuggled into England and soon was being widely circulated. He moved to Belgium in 1534 where he was arrested and imprisoned. He was tried and convicted of heresy and was strangled and burned at the stake two years later. His final prayer was that the eyes of the King would be opened to the need for the Bible to be placed in the hands of all believers and not just the clergy.

Why: His New Testament, although banned and burned, demonstrated the desire for an English translation in the common vernacular and inspired others to continue Tyndale's work.

One hundred thirteen

Who: Merrill F. Unger (1909-1980)

What: Born in Baltimore, Unger studied at Johns Hopkins University and Dallas Theological Seminary (DTS). During his career he served as pastor for churches in Dallas and Baltimore as well as a professor of Greek and theology at Gordon Divinity School and DTS. After his retirement in 1967 he began a highly productive phase of his life where he wrote extensively on various subjects related to the Bible and Christian living. He was also a frequent and popular lecturer in churches and schools.

Why: His scholarly yet accessible style made him an influential resource writer for the lay Christian, especially his *Unger's Bible Dictionary* and *Unger's Bible Handbook*.

One hundred fourteen

Who: Benjamin Breckinridge (B. B.) Warfield (1851-1921)

What: A noted Presbyterian theologian, writer, and educator, Warfield was born in Kentucky and studied at Princeton College and the University of Leipzeg. Ordained in 1879 he served briefly as a pastor in Baltimore before becoming professor of New Testament literature at Princeton Theological Seminary, a position he held for much of his life.

Why: His writings as editor of the *Presbyterian and Reformed Review* and in books like *The Plan of Salvation* presented a conservative view of Bible scholarship, Christian living, and theology that remains influential among Reformed believers.

One hundred fifteen

Who: Isaac Watts (1674-1748)

What: Watts is considered the father of English hymnody. Born in Southampton, England, he was a precocious child who learned to read almost as soon as he could speak and wrote verses while still a young boy. He was firmly attached to the principles of the Nonconformists, for which his father had suffered imprisonment, and was therefore compelled to decline the advantages of the great English universities, which at that time received only Church of England students. He attended instead the Dissenting academy in London. In 1705 he published his first volume of poems, *Horae Lyricae*, which was widely praised. His *Hymns and Spiritual Songs* appeared in 1707; *Psalms*, in 1719; and *Divine Songs for Children*, in 1720. He became pastor of an Independent Church in London in 1702 but was so frail due to ill health that much of the time the work of the parish was done by an assistant. He was buried in Westminster Abbey.

Why: His hymns, including classics like "When I Survey the Wondrous Cross," have encouraged believers and spread the Gospel message for more than two centuries.

One hundred sixteen

Who: Charles Wesley (1708-1788)

What: Wesley has been called "the poet of Methodism." Born in Epworth, England in 1707 he was educated at Westminster School and Oxford University, where he took his degree in 1728. It was while a student at Christ Church College that Wesley and a few associates, by strict attention to duty and exemplary conduct, won for themselves the derisive epithet of "Methodists." He was ordained a priest in the Church of England in 1735, and that same year he sailed with his brother John as a missionary to Georgia. They soon returned to England. He was not converted, according to his own convictions, until Whitsunday,

May 21, 1738. On that day he received a conscious knowledge of sins forgiven, and this event was the real beginning of his mission as the singer of Methodism. His hymns can generally be classified as hymns of Christian experience ("O for a Thousand Tongues to Sing"); invitation hymns ("Come, Sinners, to the Gospel Feast"); sanctification hymns ("O for a Heart to Praise My God"); funeral hymns ("Rejoice for a Brother Deceased"); and hymns on the love of God ("Wrestling Jacob"). He was not a singer alone, but as an itinerant preacher he was a busy and earnest co-laborer with his brother. After his marriage, in 1749, his itinerant labors were largely restricted to London and Bristol. Incredibly he wrote more than 6,500 hymns.

Why: His brother may have been the "mind" behind the Methodist church, but Charles was its "heart" – writing works that continue to inspire and edify.

One hundred seventeen
Who: John Wesley (1703-1791)

What: Wesley, the founder of Methodism, attended Oxford University in 1720 and was ordained deacon in 1725. He returned to Oxford in 1729 and became leader of the "holy club" or Methodists, which had been organized during his absence by his brother, Charles. He went to Georgia as a missionary in 1735. He returned to England at the end of two years, saying: "I went to America to convert the Indians, but O who shall convert me? Who is he that will deliver me from this evil heart of unbelief?" He had been impressed by the piety and faith of the Moravians in a storm while crossing the ocean, and they now became his spiritual guides. While attending one of their prayer meetings on May 24, 1738, he obtained the conscious knowledge of sins forgiven and of his acceptance with God. From this time until his death in 1791 he was unremitting in his labors as a preacher and organizer of the Methodist church. He traveled more than 250,000 miles and is credited with writing and preaching over 40,000 sermons.

Why: His zealous efforts and pious life produced one of the most influential Protestant denominations.

One hundred eighteen

Who: George Whitefield (1714-1770)

What: One of the great names in evangelism, Whitefield was born in Gloucester, England, and entered Oxford in 1733. Here he met Charles Wesley who shared his desire for utter commitment to Christ and for holy living. After his ordination in 1736 he began a ministry among the outcasts of society, including a fruitful campaign in the local prisons. Since his views of ministry differed with that of the established church he was not offered a position so he began open air preaching, presenting the Gospel in public gatherings to great acclaim. This early success set the stage for his life's work, which included numerous evangelistic crusades in the British Isles, Europe, and America – sparking tremendous revivals wherever he went. He eventually broke from the Wesleyan movement after embracing Calvinist doctrine and founded the Calvinistic Methodist Society.

Why: He joined Jonathan Edwards in launching the Great Awakening in America.

One hundred nineteen

Who: John Greenleaf Whittier (1807-1892)

What: Whittier, commonly known as the "Quaker Poet," was born in Haverhill, Massachusetts. Beginning life as a farm boy and village shoemaker, and with only a limited education, he entered the profession of journalism in 1828. He became that year editor of the *American Manufacturer* and, in 1830, editor of the *New England Review*. In 1836 he became Secretary of the American Anti-Slavery Society and editor of its official publication, the *Freeman*. In his religious poems he always magnified the goodness and love of God for humanity and the need for Christian charity. From 1824 until his death in 1892 he wrote and published poems singly in periodicals and collectively in book form. His poems include such classics as *The*

Pennsylvania Pilgrim and *Barbara Frietchie*. From these poems about 75 hymns have been made by selecting verses of religious and devotional sentiments. **Why:** He is considered one of the great American poets and the Christian themes he included in his works have brought the message of Christ to many who would not otherwise read and study religious materials.

One hundred twenty

Who: William Wilberforce (1759-1833)

What: An English abolitionist, Wilberforce was born in Yorkshire, England and studied at Cambridge. He became a member of the House of Commons in 1790 where he remained for over 30 years. Through the influence of John Newton, one of his former teachers, he became a devout evangelical Christian and an advocate for social reforms. His efforts to abolish the slave trade were achieved in 1807 when a bill that abolished the evil practice became law. His work was not done, however. It wasn't until 1833, a month after he died, that an Emancipation Bill was passed that freed all slaves under British rule. During his life he also helped to found numerous charitable organizations, mission societies, and Bible foundations.

Why: He used his power and position to help enact laws that represented the Christian ideals he believed should govern society.

One hundred twenty one

Who: John Wycliffe (c. 1329-1384)

What: Known as the first among the great Reformation figures, Wycliffe was born in Yorkshire, England and studied at Oxford, an institution he remained connected to throughout his life as a teacher and writer. When his opposition to papal abuses became known to the Vatican he was summoned before a tribunal where his ideas were condemned. His popularity was such that the pope's decree did little to subdue the desire among the general population of England to learn more about his convictions. These included the belief that the Bible is the final authority in all matters of religion, not the pope; that the pope is not infallible; that the Scriptures should be made available to all people, not just the clergy; and that the clergy should serve rather than rule the people. Despite public enthusiasm for his work, the Archbishop of London succeeded in having him suppressed and he was officially prohibited from preaching. He spent the remainder of his life writing and preparing an English translation of the Bible. At the Council of Constance in 1415 all of his surviving books that could be found were ordered burned.

Why: He ignited the spark that would blaze forth a century and a half later on October 31, 1517 when Martin Luther posted his ninety-five Theses on the church door at Wittenberg and the Protestant Reformation began in earnest.

One hundred twenty two

Who: Count (Nickolaus Ludwig) von Zinzendorf (1700-1760)

What: Count von Zinzendorf, the founder of the religious community of Herrnhut and the apostle of the United Brethren, was born in Dresden in1700. It is not often that noble blood and worldly wealth are allied with true piety and missionary zeal. Such, however, was the case with Count von Zinzendorf. In 1731 Zinzendorf resigned all public duties and devoted himself to missionary work. He traveled extensively on the Continent, in Great Britain, and in America, preaching "Christ, and him crucified," and organizing societies of Moravian brethren. John Wesley is said to have been under obligation to Zinzendorf for some ideas on singing, organization of classes, and church government. Zinzendorf was the author of some 2,000 hymns. He died at Herrnhut.

Why: He used his wealth to further the work of God's Kingdom and he helped finance many successful missionary campaigns.

One hundred twenty-three

Who: Ulrich Zwingli (1484-1531)

What: The Protestant Reformer of Switzerland, Zwingli grew up in an educated and affluent home and, at his father's bidding, studied in Vienna for the priesthood. In 1506 he was named a parish priest in Glarus where he demonstrated great skills as an orator.

When he was named chief pastor of the Great Minster Church in Zurich he began openly expressing his disagreements with the church, especially decrying such practices as the worship of Mary and the sale of indulgences. He did not fully break from Rome until he nearly died during the plague of 1519. After surviving he fully dedicated his life to the cause of spreading a unified Reformation throughout Switzerland, although he came into conflict with local Anabaptists and Lutherans over various doctrinal matters. Despite the successes he enjoined, there were many who still supported Rome. An accord, called the Peace of Kappel, was reached between the Protestants and the Catholics but by 1531 a revolt broke out and Zwingli was killed in battle. His successor was a staunch Calvinist, Johann Heinrich Bullinger, who effectively guided the Swiss church and established the Evangelical Reformed churches.

Why: His popularity made him a martyr to the Protestant cause and helped seal the success of the Reformation in Switzerland.